Our World

POLAR REGIONS

David Lambert

Silver Burdett Press
Morristown, New Jersey

Titles in this series

Deserts	Polar Regions
Jungles and Rainforests	Rivers and Lakes
Mountains	Seas and Oceans

First published in 1987 by
Wayland (Publishers) Ltd
61 Western Road, Hove
East Sussex BN3 1JD, England

Adapted and first published in the
United States in 1988 by Silver Burdett Press,
Morristown, New Jersey

© Copyright 1987 Wayland (Publishers) Ltd

Edited by Philippa Smith
US edition edited by Joanne Fink

Designed by Malcolm Smythe and Alison Leggate

Typeset by DP Press, Sevenoaks, Kent
Printed in Italy by G. Canale & C.S.p.A., Turin

Library of Congress Cataloging-in-Publication Data

Lambert, David, 1932–
   Polar regions.

   (Our World)
   Bibliography: p.
   Includes index.
   Summary: Describes the origins, geographic features, seasons,
plant and animal life, exploration, and natural resources of the
Arctic and Antarctic.
   1. Polar regions—Juvenile literature.
   [1. Polar regions]   I. Title.   II. Series.
   G590.L3   1987   919.8   87–20683
ISBN 0–382–09502–2 (lib. bdg.)

Front cover, main picture Antarctic landscape.
Front cover, inset A polar bear climbs onto an ice floe.
Polar bears are found in all Arctic areas where there is
pack ice. They spend most of their lives on the mobile ice
floes.

Back cover A scientist in Antarctica marks the egg of
an Adélie penguin.

Contents

Chapter 1   Farthest north and south

Lands of ice and snow	4
Arctic and Antarctic	6
How polar regions formed	8

Chapter 2   Land and sea

Ice sheets and glaciers	10
Mountains and valleys	12
Polar plains	14
Polar oceans	16

Chapter 3   Seasons

Summer	18
Winter	20

Chapter 4   Life in polar regions

Polar plants	22
Animals of Arctic lands	24
Arctic ocean life	26
Life in the far south	28

Chapter 5   People and polar regions

Polar peoples	30
Exploring the Arctic	32
Exploring Antarctica	34

Chapter 6   Using polar regions

Food, furs, and minerals	36
Transportation	38

Chapter 7   Protecting the Poles

Poles at risk	40
Saving the Poles	42

Glossary	45
Further reading	46
Index	47

Lands of ice and snow

Polar regions are the cold lands and seas around the North and South Poles, which are the places that mark the northernmost and southernmost points on earth. The north polar region is called the Arctic, from the Greek work *arktos* meaning "bear", for the far north lies below a bear-shaped group of stars. South polar regions form the Antarctic, a name meaning "opposite the Arctic".

The north and the south magnetic poles also lie within the polar regions. These poles are constantly moving and they do not lie in the same place as the geographic Poles.

The Arctic and Antarctic Circles are imaginary lines around the northern and southern parts of the world. The Arctic Circle is at latitude 66°32'N, while the Antarctic Circle is at 66° 32'S. They mark the approximate limits of the polar regions.

The Poles are cold partly because the sun only ever shines down upon them slantingly from low in the sky, which means that the sunshine must pass through a thick air layer before it hits the Poles. This layer of atmosphere soaks up much of the heat in sunshine, leaving less to warm the earth below. Also, because of the low angle of the sun, the same amount of sunlight covers a much larger area of the surface of the earth at the Poles than at the equator. The sunlight is therefore much weaker at the Poles. In winter, the Poles become far colder still. Then

Mist and reflections on the calm waters of Lemaire Channel, Antarctica.

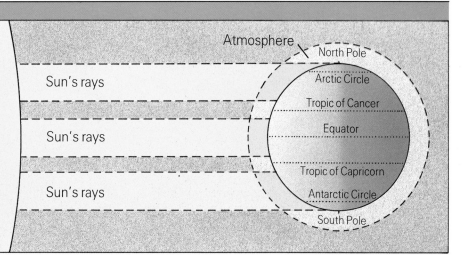

Polar sunlight
The sun's rays are less intense at the Poles than at the equator because the curvature of the earth causes the same amount of sunlight to be spread over a wider area. Also, the sun's rays pass through a greater thickness of atmosphere at the Poles, which absorbs more of the sun's heat before it reaches the earth.

Atmosphere
North Pole
Arctic Circle
Tropic of Cancer
Equator
Tropic of Capricorn
Antarctic Circle
South Pole
Sun's rays
Sun's rays
Sun's rays

the sun does not rise at all for months, and the land and sea lose heat into the sky.

Polar regions are among the harshest places in the world. Bitterly cold winter lasts for more than half the year, and strong winds make winter temperatures feel even lower than they are. Anyone not very well bundled up could freeze to death in minutes in a polar winter gale. Polar summers are short and cool, and frost and snow can come at any time of year.

Huge tracts of Arctic and Antarctic land or sea always lie under snow or ice. Yet in most places so little snow or rain falls in a year that geographers call polar regions frozen deserts. But where snow has melted the ground is wet and boggy, and here, hardy plants and animals can thrive.

Right During the long Arctic winter, violent storms are frequent.

Water, land, and ice
70.8% of the earth's surface is covered by water, and the remaining 29.2% is land. This diagram shows the proportions of the earth's surface that are under ice.

Water 62.3%

Land 26.3%

Frozen water 8.5%

Land under ice 2.9%

Arctic and Antarctic

The Arctic is mostly ocean surrounded by land. The Antarctic is land surrounded by ocean.

The Arctic Ocean lies north of Asia, North America, and Europe. This partly frozen ocean is larger than all Europe. Around the ocean's rim lie scores of islands. One is Greenland, often called the largest island in the world. Groups of islands divide parts of the Arctic Ocean into seas, bays, and narrow strips of water. Water gaps also join the Arctic Ocean with the warmer Pacific and Atlantic Oceans to its south.

As well as Greenland, Arctic lands include northern regions of Alaska, Canada, Scandinavia, Finland, and the Soviet Union. A world map shows Arctic lands as a narrow rim north of the Arctic Circle. Not all places north of this are very cold. In winter, mild ocean currents keep part of Arctic Norway no colder than New York. Yet Canada's Hudson Bay, far south of the Arctic Circle, is colder than some islands near the North Pole.

Many people consider that the tree line is a truer limit to Arctic lands. This line marks the farthest north that trees will grow. Beyond this it is too cold. The map below shows this tree line wriggling north and south of the Arctic Circle.

In the far south lies the world's fifth largest continent, Antarctica, which is almost twice the size of Australia. Antarctica looks like a fat tadpole with a curly tail, but its true shape and size are hidden under ice. Scientists believe that East

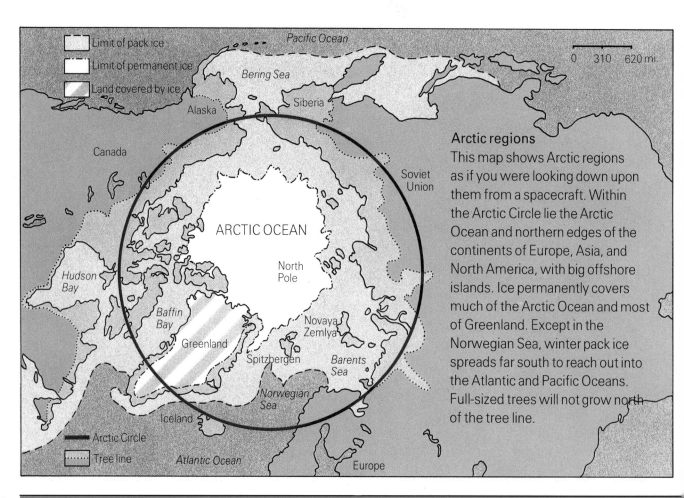

Arctic regions
This map shows Arctic regions as if you were looking down upon them from a spacecraft. Within the Arctic Circle lie the Arctic Ocean and northern edges of the continents of Europe, Asia, and North America, with big offshore islands. Ice permanently covers much of the Arctic Ocean and most of Greenland. Except in the Norwegian Sea, winter pack ice spreads far south to reach out into the Atlantic and Pacific Oceans. Full-sized trees will not grow north of the tree line.

Antarctica — the tadpole's body — is high tableland, while West Antarctica — the tail — is a line of mountainous islands joined by ice.

Most of Antarctica lies south of the Antarctic Circle, and all is very cold. Cold sea surrounds this frozen land. Southern parts of the Atlantic, Indian, and Pacific Oceans form these Antarctic waters, which are colder and less salty than ocean water farther north. North of the Antarctic Circle, the meeting place of cold and warmer water is known as the Antarctic Convergence. This shifting line is where Antarctic regions end.

Left *Inuit* hunting seals from their sealskin kayaks off the coast of Greenland.

Antarctic regions

This map shows the cold land and ocean that make up the Antarctic. While the Arctic consists of an ocean almost surrounded by three continents, the Antarctic is a continent surrounded by three oceans: the southern parts of the Atlantic, Indian, and Pacific Oceans. Some people call the chilly southern waters the Southern Ocean. The great cold continent of Antarctica takes up most of the area inside the Antarctic Circle. From parts of Antarctica, ice always juts into the sea. In winter, pack ice extends much farther still. The Antarctic Convergence, the limit of Antarctic regions, lies outside the pack-ice boundary, so does not fit inside our map.

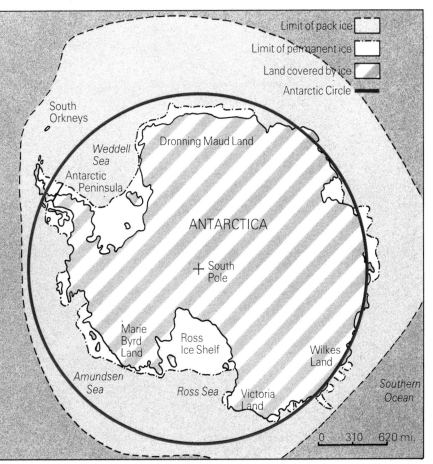

How polar regions formed

The polar regions have not always been cold. Hundreds of millions of years ago the sun shone down hotly on what are now Antarctica and Arctic lands. Lush tropical forests sprouted in steamy swamps where large prehistoric beasts lived. Greenland was the home of *Ichthyostega*, a big, sprawling early relative of salamanders and newts. Much later, *Lystrosaurus*, a hippopotamus-like reptile, lived in Antarctica. Scientists have learned all this from rocks containing fossils of these long-dead animals and plants.

Other clues show that what are now the polar lands were once warm because they lay near the equator. They cooled down only after drifting north or south on currents in the sticky, molten rock that lies below continents and ocean floors.

By 50 million years ago all continents had reached the places where they lie today. Ocean currents could no longer spread warmth south of the Antarctic Circle because Antarctica stood in the way. At the same time, Europe, Asia, and North America blocked ocean currents bringing warmth to the far north. So Arctic and Antarctic regions started cooling down. In winter, snow fell and ice formed on the sea. Even summer was not always warm enough to melt all winter snow and ice. Some lingered and reflected sunshine back into the sky, so that sea and land grew colder still.

By five million years ago a crust of ice covered almost all Antarctica. By three million years ago Arctic lands were disappearing under caps of ice. So began the ice age that we live in now. At times, snow and ice have spread far out beyond the polar regions. Great ice sheets once covered all Canada, part of the United States, the British Isles, Scandinavia, and much of the Soviet Union.

At other times, enough heat reached northern lands to make most ice caps melt. We live in just such a warm break in the present ice age. But some scientists believe that, within a thousand years or so, polar cold will spread again. Experts think that polar lands themselves will not warm up until they drift outside the Arctic and Antarctic Circles, and that will not be for many millions of years.

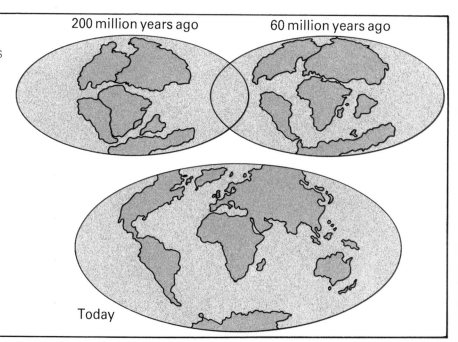

Shifting continents
Three views show how the earth's continents have shifted in the last 200 million years.

About 200 million years ago most land belonged to one huge, warm continent, but smaller continents were splitting off.

By 60 million years ago, wide ocean gaps separated most continents. Some drifted north or south toward the poles.

Today, land rings the North Pole and covers the South Pole. Warm ocean water no longer reaches polar regions.

200 million years ago

60 million years ago

Today

Left Different ages of sea ice off the Greenland coast.

Below Prehistoric beasts once inhabited warm, swampy lands where polar regions are today. About 220 million years ago, this hippo-like reptile, *Lystrosaurus*, roamed Antarctica and some other southern continents. *Lystrosaurus* grew to three feet in length.

Ice sheets and glaciers

Much polar land is always buried under ice. This ice has formed from snow squashed by the weight of later snowfalls pressing on it from above. In time some ice sheets grow immensely thick and wide. The Antarctic ice sheet — the world's largest — is bigger than any country except the Soviet Union. Antarctica's great icy lid is up to 14,000 feet thick, but more than half of that thickness lies below the sea, for the great weight of ice has pushed down the surface of the land that lies beneath it. The Antarctic ice sheet is seven times bigger than the Greenland ice sheet, the largest in the northern hemisphere. But even Greenland's ice sheet could cover the huge country of Libya. Smaller coats of ice, called ice caps, hide high parts of Spitzbergen, Novaya Zemlya, and other Arctic islands.

An ice sheet's surface is largely smooth and snowy. But in places there are long, straight, knee-high ridges called sastrugi. These develop when a strong wind blows steadily from one direction, heaping up the snow like sand dunes in a desert.

Ice sheets do not lie still. From the high central areas of Antarctica and Greenland great tongues of ice, called glaciers, creep down toward the sea. Glaciers also develop high up on polar islands, then flow down through valleys created by rivers long ago. The longest glaciers are very long indeed. Eight of the polar glaciers measure at least 125 miles.

The middle of a glacier moves faster than the sides. This sets up strains that split the surface with deep cracks called crevasses. Most glaciers flow at a rate slower than one pace a day. A snowflake falling in the middle of Greenland may take 3,000 years to reach the sea.

Some mountain glaciers melt when they reach mild air, low down, but many polar glaciers end only where they plunge into the sea.

Right The massive Victoria Land Glacier in Antarctica flowing into the sea.

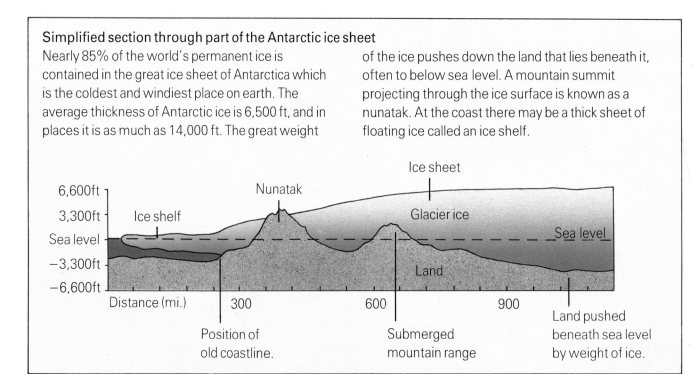

Simplified section through part of the Antarctic ice sheet

Nearly 85% of the world's permanent ice is contained in the great ice sheet of Antarctica which is the coldest and windiest place on earth. The average thickness of Antarctic ice is 6,500 ft, and in places it is as much as 14,000 ft. The great weight of the ice pushes down the land that lies beneath it, often to below sea level. A mountain summit projecting through the ice surface is known as a nunatak. At the coast there may be a thick sheet of floating ice called an ice shelf.

Mountains and valleys

Frost and ice shape polar peaks and valleys. In places ice is wearing away the land. On bare mountainsides freezing water fills cracks in the rock and forces the cracks wider. This splits off slabs that fall downhill to pile up on the ground as stony heaps called scree. Ice also fills and deepens hollows high on mountain slopes. Where ice creates hollows on two sides of a mountain, the top between the two is worn back into a sharp ridge called an arête. If three hollows almost meet they gnaw the mountain top into a pyramid. Here and there, sharp rocky peaks and ridges poke above the world's great ice sheets like islands in a frozen sea. These rocky peaks are called nunataks.

Ice also shapes the land buried under glaciers and ice sheets. Loose stones stuck in the bottom of the moving ice rub away and smooth the solid rock beneath. As a glacier creeps down a valley, it chops off ridges jutting from the valley sides and makes the valley floor much deeper. Where some glaciers

Above Pyramidal peaks in the southwest corner of Denali National Park in Alaska.

Rock debris (moraine) frozen into a glacier in eastern Greenland.

Glaciated valleys

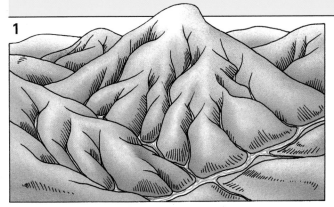

1. These mountain valleys were shaped by rivers that wore away the mountainsides. Both sides of each valley slope down toward the middle like a letter V.

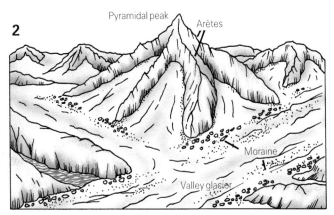

Pyramidal peak

Arêtes

Moraine

Valley glacier

2. Glaciers have filled the largest valleys and cut into the mountainsides. Broken rock has fallen on the glaciers in lines of rubble called moraines.

Hanging valley

Cirque

Scree

3. The glaciers have melted. But they have left the valleys widened and deepened. The main valley now curves down toward the middle like a letter U.

have melted, the sea floods the valley floors to form long, deep, steep-sided inlets called fjords.

As glaciers and ice sheets melt they shed the huge loads of broken rocks they have been carrying. Boulders as big as cottages lie scattered on Arctic lands where they were dumped when the ice sheets melted thousands of years ago. Here, too, you find large masses of stones, sand, and clay called till, which sometimes take the shape of drumlins — rows of hillocks like giant eggs lying in a basket. Drumlins probably formed beneath ice sheets. Walls of stony rubble, called end moraines, lie across some Arctic valley floors. These stones fell from the melting snouts of valley glaciers.

Where streams flowed out from underneath a melting ice sheet they spread sheets of sand and gravel far across the Arctic countryside. Here, too, you find long, winding sand and gravel ridges known as eskers, which are deposited by streams flowing under the ice.

Below Large boulders carried far from their place of origin by glacier ice long ago are called erratics.

Polar plains

Vast treeless lowlands, called tundra, sprawl across much of Arctic North America and Soviet Union. *Tundra* is a Finnish word for "barren land". In winter the tundra wears a snowy blanket, except where winds have swept low hilltops bare. When the snow melts you see plains, with lakes, bogs, loose stones, and stretches of bare rock.

Parts of the tundra were scraped bare of soil by ice sheets long ago. From the air, much of Canada's Northwest Territories look like a huge flat slab, with ice-worn grooves now filled by countless narrow lakes.

Much Arctic lowland has a covering of blue-gray soil and loose stones. The surface melts each summer but the ground below stays frozen all year long. This ever-frozen rock and subsoil is called permafrost. In places permafrost is more than 4,500 feet thick. Permafrost extends south of the Arctic into northern forest lands. In fact scientists think frozen soil or rock lie below one-fifth of the world's land surface.

Permafrost helps shape the ground above. In summer this is boggy because melted snow and ice cannot soak into the frozen ground below. On even gentle slopes, loose soil and rocks slowly slide downhill on top of frozen subsoil.

Some of the strangest tundra sights are hillocks known as pingos. Pingos may be up to 295 feet high. Each stands where an ice plug formed below an empty lake, pushing up the lake floor like a monstrous blister.

Between them, frost and permafrost sort stones into patterns. Stone circles start as cracks that open up in muddy ground which has dried and shrunk. Later, the freezing process pushes stones sideways until they fill the cracks.

Below A pingo in eastern Greenland.

Tundra vegetation in autumn in McKinley National Park, Alaska. In the distance Mount McKinley, the highest peak in North America, soars to 20,320 feet.

Polar oceans

Gleaming sheets and slabs of ice cover a huge part of the Arctic Ocean and fringe Antarctica. Most ice has formed where the sea has frozen over. But much ice has spread into the sea from the land. Polar sea ice shrinks in summer but spreads in winter, so that Antarctica seems to double in size.

As summer ends, new sea ice first forms in river mouths and sheltered bays. Here a thin ice crust soon covers the surface of the sea. Even if it is thick enough to walk on, this coating of young ice will bend beneath your weight. Storms and tides can break it into slabs, called pancake ice because they look like giant pancakes. As the sea grows colder, pancakes clump together and thicken. Most sea ice grows no more than 6.5 feet thick, but storms drive slabs of ice on top of one another. Their edges rear up, producing high pressure ridges and a tumbled mass of blocks. This is called pack ice.

On a winter journey from the Arctic tundra to the North Pole you would start by crossing fast ice — sea ice stuck to land. Then comes a strip of open water called a shore lead, or polynya. Winds, tides, and currents help to keep this water open. Beyond lie slabs of pack ice glued together by their pressure ridges. Each summer most fast ice and much pack ice melts. But a thick roof of ancient polar ice

An ice-bound polar coast

From a low shore, fast ice juts out into the sea. Here and there, this ice is split by strips of open water called shore leads, and areas of open water in the pack ice called polynyas. Where a steep-sided valley meets the sea, a glacier sheds huge chunks of ice that fall into the sea and float away as icebergs.

Fast ice

Shore lead

Glacier

Pack ice

Polynya

Iceberg

always crowns the middle of the Arctic Ocean. Pack ice and polar ice are never still. Winds and currents slowly move them around the Arctic Ocean.

Meanwhile glaciers are always adding new ice to the sea. Around Greenland, great chunks of ice plunge from the ends of valley glaciers and float away as towering icebergs shaped like castles. Around Antarctica, flat-topped icebergs break off from ice shelves jutting out into the sea. The biggest icebergs can drift far beyond the polar regions before they melt away entirely.

Left Pancake ice off the shores of Antarctica.

Below Crabeater seals swimming under the ice near the South Orkneys in Antarctica.

Summer

At the North Pole the sun rises in late March and does not set until late September. At the South Pole it is daylight from September to March. Yet polar summers are short and mostly cool or cold, as the sun never shines down from high overhead. On ice sheets, much of the sunshine is reflected back into the sky so it cannot heat the ground. Elsewhere, sunshine takes time to melt snow and ice before warming land, sea, and air.

Arctic summer starts in June and ends in August or September. There is scarcely any spring or autumn. All Arctic plants and animals are adapted to make maximum use of the short summer. Inside the Arctic, the tundra has the warmest summers. On Canada's cold Arctic islands, snow starts to thaw in late May and much has gone by early July. By late July, sea ice is breaking up.

Mainland Canada and Siberia enjoy calm weeks of unbroken summer sunshine. Here it feels quite hot at times. But the warmest Arctic month averages only 50 °F. Sunny spells can end in thunderstorms, but generally there is little rain.

Arctic seas have colder, cloudier summers. As damp air passes over ice, its moisture condenses into fogs and sheets of low, drizzling cloud. In summer, Arctic seas are among the cloudiest places on earth. Over the Arctic pack ice the air is seldom much above freezing.

On the world's great ice sheets summer never really comes at all. Greenland's warmest month averages a bitterly cold −12 °F. Most of Antarctica is even colder. Summer on the high Antarctic plateau feels as chilly as midwinter in the colder Arctic regions. Even Antarctic coasts barely start to thaw, although their rim of sea ice starts to shrink.

During polar summers, cold air above the ground produces the strange effects called mirages. In a cold-weather mirage, cold air above the ground bends light from distant mountains so that they seem to float in the sky.

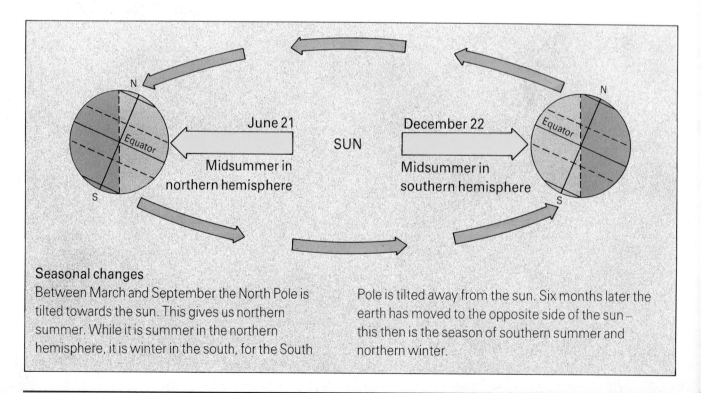

Seasonal changes
Between March and September the North Pole is tilted towards the sun. This gives us northern summer. While it is summer in the northern hemisphere, it is winter in the south, for the South Pole is tilted away from the sun. Six months later the earth has moved to the opposite side of the sun – this then is the season of southern summer and northern winter.

The midnight sun in Greenland. In the Arctic summer there is almost continuous daylight during May, June, and July.

Winter

Winter is the longest polar season. It lasts for eight or nine months of the year.

In the Arctic, winter starts in August or September. As the sun dips lower in the sky, the rims of lakes and seas begin to freeze. At the North Pole the sun sinks below the horizon in late September and does not rise again until late March. Without sunshine to warm them, land and sea soon grow very cold indeed. But some Arctic areas grow chillier than others. The mildest parts are those touched by Atlantic or Pacific Ocean waters. Here, the temperature falls only just below freezing even in January, the coldest month. But moist ocean winds bring winter storms and heavy snowfall to these regions.

Much colder, drier, quieter air covers the Arctic Ocean shores of Alaska, Canada, and Siberia, and the central Arctic Ocean. Summer warmth stored in the surface of the ground is soon lost into a cloudless sky. At Verkhoyansk in northeast Siberia, the temperature once plunged to $-89.9\,°F$, the lowest ever measured in the northern hemisphere.

The coldest, harshest winters anywhere are those that grip Antarctica. High up on the Antarctic

Midwinter midnight at one of the research bases in Antarctica.

ice sheet in July 1983 the temperature sank to a world record low of −128.6 °F. Even Antarctic coasts endure much colder winters than Arctic shores. Antarctic winds are fiercer, too. Cold, heavy air pours off the inland ice sheet, and gales whirl around the continent, whipping up snow from the ground to form blizzards.

Yet polar winters can be beautiful. As winter starts and ends, weeks of twilight keep the sky aglow. Even in midwinter, moonlight is reflected brightly off the snow and ice. And sometimes colored curtains of light, called auroras, shimmer high up in the atmosphere.

Above The aurora borealis, or "northern lights" are sometimes seen in a winter's sky in Arctic regions.

Below A moonlit iceberg on a calm winter's night.

Polar plants

Only low-growing hardy plants with shallow roots can live in polar regions. All others would be killed by long, harsh winters, chilly summers, poor soils, or permafrost.

Polar plants have ways of coping with these problems. Some have sap like antifreeze to stop stems from freezing through and bursting open. Many, like the ground willow, hug the ground, where cold winds cannot dry them out or batter tender shoots with snow and sand. Although a ground willow may have branches up to 16 feet in length, they may never rise more than 4 inches above the ground. The furry stems of Arctic poppies trap air, which helps stop them from losing moisture. Saxifrages form low, tight cushions that trap the sun's heat even when the air is icy cold.

Most polar plants live for years but grow for only two months of every twelve. These perennials mainly spread from creeping underground shoots that put out buds. There are few annuals — plants that spring from seeds and only live a year. The growing season is too short for most of them to sprout and for their seeds to ripen.

Different types of polar landscapes have special sets of plants. Only mosses and lichens grow among the bare rocks farthest north. The lichens look like red and yellow stains on the rock. Some grow so slowly that they have taken perhaps 4,000 years to form.

Farther south you find a richer vegetation. In summer, large stretches of the tundra are bright with flowers or green with heather, berry plants, and tiny knee-high trees. Most are willows and birches. There are also 400-year-old junipers with only thumb-thick stems. No tree grows tall, for winter winds kill any shoots that poke above the snow. Wet, boggy ground is a waving sea of cotton grass above a soggy blanket of sphagnum moss.

Only two flowering plants — a grass and a pink — cling to the edge of intensely cold Antarctica. Here, though, tiny, reddish types of the lowly plants called algae give melting snow a rosy glow.

Arctic plants

These low-growing , seed-producing plants manage to survive in the harsh climate of the far north.
They may be found in damp hollows, on south-facing slopes and on patches of soil protected from the wind.

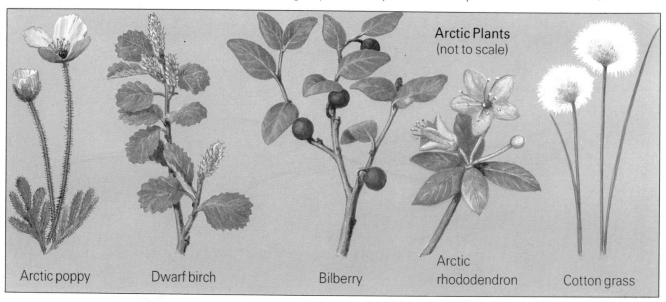

Arctic Plants
(not to scale)

Arctic poppy   Dwarf birch   Bilberry   Arctic rhododendron   Cotton grass

Left Purple mountain saxifrage, common in Arctic Canada and Greenland, provides a splash of color during the short polar summer.

Most rock surfaces on Signy Island in Antarctica are mottled with colorful lichens.

Animals of Arctic lands

Animals of far northern lands have to solve two problems: surviving the cold and finding food.

Most Arctic land animals are warm-blooded creatures that trap body heat with help from fur or feathers. Short underwool and long guard hairs keep Arctic foxes comfortably warm even at temperatures as low as −40° F. Musk oxen grow long thick winter coats that almost touch the ground. Birds called ptarmigan have feathered feet that help them stay warm. Stoats' coats turn white in winter. This helps to keep them warm, for the hollow white hairs hold air instead of pigment (coloring substance), and trapped air insulates them against the cold. The hollow hairs of European reindeer and American caribou (two names for one kind of animal) provide among the warmest of all clothing materials.

In winter food is often difficult to find, but the little rodents called lemmings dig tunnels under snow in search of berries, roots, and stems. Foxes, weasels, stoats, or snowy owls will pounce on any lemmings they can catch. Stoats, foxes, wolves, and wolverines also hunt Arctic hares, and wolves attack caribou far larger than themselves.

Summer

These creatures find plenty to eat in the long summer days of the North American Arctic. Sandhill cranes and whistling swans fly far to feed and breed here, and caribou trek from forests south of the Arctic.

Musk oxen and Arctic foxes live here all the year, as do Arctic ground squirrels, the only Arctic mammals that hibernate in winter.

Caribou (reindeer)

Musk oxen

Sandhill crane

Arctic fox

Whistling swans

Arctic ground squirrel

A few kinds of mammals and most birds would starve if they spent winter in the Arctic, so they migrate away from polar regions. As summer ends, huge herds of caribou trek far south to graze on forest lichens, while overhead, ducks, geese, and songbirds fly south as well. Next spring, all these animals will return to breed and feed on tundra plants, fish, or insects newly-hatched from eggs.

In years when food is plentiful, hares and lemmings quickly multiply. So do the owls and foxes that prey upon them. But after a while there are more plant-eaters than plants for them to eat. Most starve to death, together with most of their predators.

Winter

The creatures shown on this page manage to keep warm and find food all through an Arctic winter. The Arctic fox and Arctic hare have thick white winter coats, making it hard for these enemies to see each other in the snow. Voles and lemmings hide in burrows dug in the snow. But weasels are slender enough to chase them down their holes. Their warm winter coats give these little rodents no protection against a weasel's sharp teeth and claws.

Arctic hares

Arctic fox

Weasel

Tundra vole

Arctic lemming

Arctic ocean life

The Arctic Ocean's icy rim teems with living things. for here the waters are full of nutrients and oxygen. All animals eat plants or one another, so plants and animals form food chains whose links are the eaters and the eaten.

Billions of tiny plants called algae grow on the underside of floating ice. Billions more tiny floating plants make up the phytoplankton.

Tiny shrimplike amphipods graze on algae-covered underwater ice. Even smaller animals called copepods eat phytoplankton. Copepods themselves form food for other creatures living in the phytoplankton. Together, these billions of small drifting animals are known as zooplankton.

Zooplankton is eaten by small fish and some much larger animals. (The blue whale, the largest creature on earth, swims open-mouthed through clouds of shrimplike creatures known as krill.)

Small fish, in their turn, are snapped up by larger relatives, such as the polar cod and Arctic char.

Big sea mammals, such as the white whale and several kinds of northern seal, catch fish underwater, while the walrus rakes shellfish from the seabed with its tusks.

Even animals as large as these fall prey to more ferocious hunters. Polar bears hunt seals on pack ice. A bear will wait beside a seal's breathing hole in the ice, and snatch the seal the next time it surfaces to breathe. Polar bears swim far across the sea to reach new feeding grounds. Their oily, waterproof fur keeps them warm in the icy water.

Apart from polar bears and people, killer whales are the most ferocious hunters of polar seas. These big black and white whales eat mainly fish and squid. But packs of killer whales will also hunt and kill seals and other species of whale.

Left The beluga, or white whale, is found in Arctic waters north of the Arctic Circle, especially in areas close to river mouths.

Right Walrus are large animals protected from the cold by thick layers of blubber. They use their long tusks to gather food from the seabed.

Life in the far south

Most animals that live on harsh Antarctica are tiny. Threadworms, mites, wingless flies, and little jumping insects called springtails, manage to survive the cold. Yet no backboned animals spend their lives upon this frozen continent. Millions of seabirds and big sea mammals do come ashore upon Antarctica or nearby islands to rest or breed, but almost all feed in the sea.

Five kinds of seal swim off Antarctic shores. Crabeater seals catch krill. Ross seals swim under the ice to capture cuttlefish and fish such as the Antarctic cod, a fish whose blood contains chemicals that keep it from freezing. Weddell seals dive to a depth of 1,800 feet to hunt seabed fish. Leopard seals lie in wait for penguins. Elephant seals feed on squid. The males are the largest seals of all: up to half as heavy as an elephant.

At sea all seals swim quickly and gracefully. On land, they can only hump themselves along slowly, for their limbs are short, stubby, and flipper-shaped. In air or water, thick body fat keeps out the cold.

Millions of penguins live in and near Antarctic waters. These flightless birds can only use their wings as flippers. But they are expert swimmers, catching squid or fish. If danger threatens, the small Adélie penguin can leap up almost 6.5 feet, straight out of the sea onto a shelf of ice.

On land, penguins waddle upright and look like short, plump men wearing dinner jackets. When moving downhill they can travel faster by sliding on their bellies.

Most penguins come ashore to breed in spring. But the hardy emperor penguin — the biggest penguin — lays her one egg on an ice sheet in the darkness of Antarctic winter. For months the males incubate eggs between their feet and belly skin flaps. Meanwhile the females catch squid at sea on which they feed their babies when the eggs hatch.

Left A Weddell seal with her two-week-old twins.

Right A gentoo penguin feeds two chicks. Gentoo penguins nest in vast, crowded rookeries. Their nests are made from small pebbles. Although awkward on land, these penguins can swim at speeds of up to 25 mph underwater.

Polar peoples

For centuries, the hardy, nomadic peoples living on tundra lands around the Arctic rim have survived the cold and won food from lands where crops won't grow. Now only about 800,000 remain.

The Lapps, a strong, dark-haired people, inhabit the shores and mountains of north Sweden and its north European neighbors. Some northern Lapps live and wander with large herds of reindeer. These animals provide the herdsmen with meat and milk, and Lapps make warm clothing from reindeer skins.

Farther east such people as the Samoyeds and Yakuts live in the Arctic regions of the Soviet Union. Some Samoyeds herd reindeer, and fish and hunt for food. The Yakuts of the northeast raise cattle, but have to bring them extra food in winter when grass is scarce.

The most famous of all Arctic peoples are those we know as Eskimos, an Indian name the Eskimos themselves dislike because it just means "eaters of raw meat". The Eskimos call themselves *Inuit* or

A Lapp reindeer herder feeds a weak reindeer calf.

Building an igloo

The pictures show four stages in building an *Inuit* winter snowhouse.

(1) Hard-packed snow is cut into blocks up to 3 ft. in length. These are stood on edge to make a low round wall up to 10 ft. across. Part of the wall will be cut away to make a slope.

(2) New blocks are built up this slope.

(3) More blocks are added to form a spiral that grows smaller as it rises, and so builds the wall into a low, domed room.

(4) A snow tunnel lets in people but traps cold air. A small hole on top lets out smoke from a fire. Some igloos have ice slabs as windows. Inside, people sleep on a platform of snow.

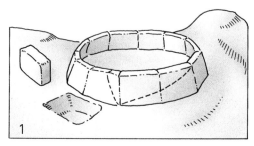

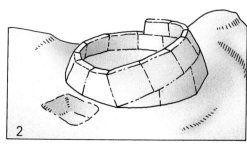

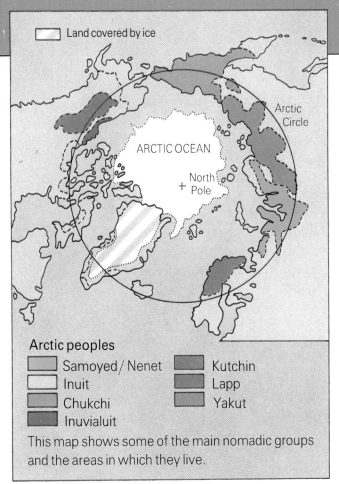

Land covered by ice

ARCTIC OCEAN

North Pole +

Arctic Circle

Arctic peoples

Samoyed / Nenet
Inuit
Chukchi
Inuvialuit
Kutchin
Lapp
Yakut

This map shows some of the main nomadic groups and the areas in which they live.

"the people". They live in the North American Arctic and in Greenland.

Long ago, the *Inuit* learned to catch and kill seals, whales, polar bears, and caribou for food and clothing. Hunters harpooned sea mammals from sealskin canoes called kayaks. They traveled over snow on sledges, built largely of bone and hide and pulled by dogs. Everyone wore hooded jackets, trousers, boots, and mittens made of animal skins stitched with animal sinews. In summer the *Inuit* lived in sealskin tents. In winter they sheltered from the cold in turf huts or small domed houses made of blocks of snow.

This ancient way of life has almost disappeared. Most *Inuit* now live in modern homes and shop in stores. Some work in factories or mines.

Modern ways of life have even reached remote Antarctica But the only people there are scientists, most of whom stay only for months not years.

Below An *Inuit* lights a stove inside his igloo.

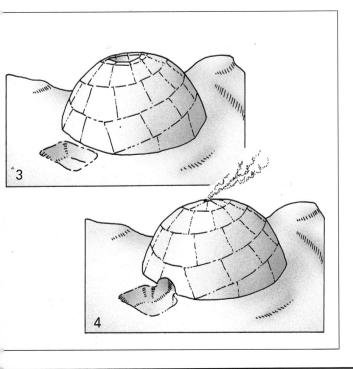

3

4

Exploring the Arctic

Early explorers of the Arctic included ancestors of the *Inuit*. These Stone Age peoples reached this frozen region thousands of years ago. But they left no written record of their journeys. In the warm southern lands of Europe, the ancient Greeks and Romans believed no one could live in the icy north.

By AD 1000, adventurous Norwegian sailors had found and peopled southern Greenland. Yet it was much later before Europeans seriously probed the Arctic. From the late 1500s onward they came in search of new sea routes to Asia. Some sought a northwest passage around northern North America. Others tried to find a northeast passage by way of northern Europe. At first they all found that sea ice blocked their way or crushed their fragile sailing ships. Many died of cold, disease, or hunger.

Success came slowly. At last, in 1879, Sweden's Nils Nordenskjold sailed right around northern Europe and north Asia and thus completed the Northeast Passage. By 1906, Roald Amundsen of Norway had managed to complete the Northwest Passage. While in Canada and the Soviet Union, fur traders reached the Arctic Ocean overland.

By the early 1900s, adventurers competed with each other to be first to reach the North Pole itself. Robert Peary of the U.S. Navy is credited with winning the race in 1909. Peary used sledges pulled by dogs to cross the frozen Arctic Ocean.

Since then, aircraft, submarines, icebreakers, and artificial satellites have made it easier to unlock the secrets of the frozen north. (In 1958, the U.S. submarine *Nautilus* reached the pole itself from below.) Arctic shores and seas have now been mapped. But much more remains to be discovered. Today's explorers are the scientists who come to study the rocks, minerals, weather, ocean currents, and wildlife of the north.

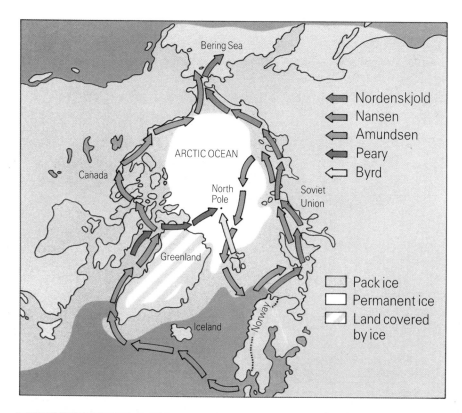

Legend:
← Nordenskjold
← Nansen
← Amundsen
← Peary
⇐ Byrd

☐ Pack ice
☐ Permanent ice
▨ Land covered by ice

Arctic explorers' routes

This map shows the routes of five Arctic explorers. Nils Nordenskjold's voyage from Norway to the Bering Sea in 1879 completed the first Northeast Passage. Fridtjof Nansen's drift voyage locked in ice took him near the North Pole (1893–96). Roald Amundsen coasted along Arctic Canada to complete the first Northwest Passage (1906). From Greenland, Robert Peary trekked over ice to the North Pole (1909). Richard Byrd claimed to have flown to the North Pole in 1926.

Martin Frobisher was one of many sixteenth-century European explorers to search for a northwest passage. Here, members of his expedition clash with *Inuit* off the coast of Greenland.

Below right Robert Peary, of the U.S. Navy, led an expedition to the North Pole in 1909. Here he has set up camp on sea ice.

Below left Fridtjof Nansen was a famous Norwegian explorer. This picture, taken in 1895, shows his ship, the *Fram*, frozen into Arctic ice.

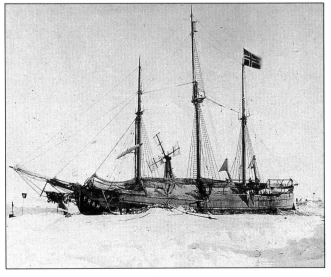

Exploring Antarctica

Antarctica was the last continent to be discovered and explored, although people long suspected it lay there. From 1773 to 1774 the British explorer James Cook sailed around Antarctica but never saw it. His frail ship could not break through the fringing ice. Between 1800 and 1820 seal hunters glimpsed Antarctica. In 1821 an American seal hunter, Captain John Davis, sent men ashore on the Antarctic Peninsula. These were the first to land there. Then, in 1840, Lieutenant Charles Wilkes of the U.S. Navy sailed far enough along the coast to prove that Antarctica was a single mass of land and ice.

But it was not until the early 1900s that scientists and explorers began to probe the vast ice sheet and its glaciers. In 1911, Norway's Roald Amundsen, with dog teams pulling sledges, raced the British explorer Robert Falcon Scott to the South Pole — and won. Scott reached the Pole on foot, but all five in his expedition team died of cold and hunger.

Since then, planes, radios, and snow tractors have made Antarctic exploration much quicker, easier and safer. Between the 1920s and 1950s, Richard Byrd of the U.S. Navy led big expeditions to map Antarctica and learn about its weather, rocks, and ice. In 1957, twelve nations sent teams of scientists who set up forty camps upon the continent. That year Vivian Fuchs led a British Commonwealth expedition which became the first to cross Antarctica on land.

Now, New Zealand, Britain, Chile, the Soviet Union, the United States and more than half a dozen other countries keep teams of scientists at work in Antarctica. Many stay in comfortable camps manned all year round. Between them, experts study everything from seals to ice. By 1984 the Soviets had already drilled down through 6,562 feet of the Antarctic ice sheet, but still had far to go. On this, the harshest continent on earth, much still remains to be discovered.

Scott Base, a New Zealand research station in the Antarctic, is manned all year round.

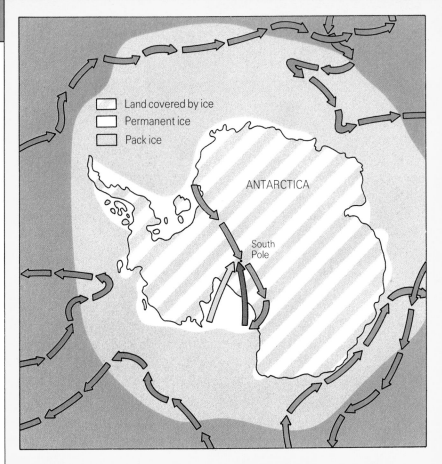

Land covered by ice
Permanent ice
Pack ice

ANTARCTICA

South
Pole

Antarctic explorers' routes

Cook Wilkes
Scott Amundsen
Trans-Antarctic Expedition

Routes of five expeditions to the far south are shown on this map. James Cook almost reached Antarctica in 1773. In 1840 Charles Wilkes sailed past a long stretch of Antarctic coast later called Wilkes Land. Roald Amundsen reached the South Pole in 1911. Robert Scott got there a month later, but never returned. Richard Byrd flew to the Pole in 1929. In 1958 Vivian Fuchs's Trans-Antarctic Expedition passed the South Pole on the first land crossing of Antarctica.

Three of Scott's South Pole expedition team, 1911.

Food, furs, and minerals

Polar regions may be too cold for growing crops, but they are rich in certain foods and minerals.

In northern Europe and north Asia, herdsmen pasture half-wild reindeer on the tundra in the summer months. Here, and in Alaska and Canada, hunters trap foxes and other Arctic creatures whose soft, furry skins make valuable coats. Fishermen set out from Iceland, Alaska, and the Arctic shores of the Soviet Union. The north's richest fisheries lie in the sub-Arctic waters of the Barents Sea, and the Atlantic Ocean off southwest Greenland, where the cold water teems with salmon, cod, halibut, and other edible fish.

In the far south, fishing fleets from lands as distant as Japan and the Soviet Union catch huge quantities of Antarctic cod. Now, too, some vessels scoop up millions of krill.

Once, sealers and whalers killed thousands of Arctic and Antarctic seals and whales for food, or for their oil which people used to burn in lamps before they had electric light. Now miners come to the Arctic for mineral oil — petroleum trapped below the Arctic's frozen soil and seas. Sometimes, engineers must drill deep down from artificial islands built in the sea itself, for drilling ships might well be crushed or pushed aside by moving ice. The work is difficult and cold, but brings rewards. Some of the richest fields of oil and natural gas lie under northern Alaska, Canada, and the Soviet Union.

Arctic rocks hold more than oil. Copper, gold, and silver come from northwestern Canada, while coal, iron, and other minerals are mined in the Arctic parts of the Soviet Union and Scandinavia.

Prospectors have proved that valuable minerals lie buried in Antarctica. The list includes coal, gold, iron ore, copper, and titanium. By the mid-1980s no one had actually tried to extract them. Today this work would cost more than these substances are worth. But one day they might become scarce enough to make the task worthwhile.

Left Setting a trap in Arctic Canada.

Top right A Lapp woman and her daughter sell reindeer skins to summer tourists.

Bottom right The Trans-Alaska oil pipeline.

Transportation

Polar travel is difficult at any time of year. In the Arctic winter, feet and wheels sink in the snow, and no ordinary ships or boats can break through the thick sea ice. (Antarctica, of course, is mostly frozen all year round.) In the Arctic summer, swamps hinder travel over land, though melting ice makes water travel easier.

Despite these problems, miners, hunters, fishermen, and others somehow get around. In winter, foot travelers can fix snowshoes shaped like tennis rackets to their feet. These spread the body's weight and stop the feet from sinking in soft snow. But you can travel faster if you slide along on skis. Skiers sometimes pull loaded sleds, but reindeer or dog teams are better at this task.

Now, though, machines are taking over. People speed around on powered snowmobiles that slide on runners, and a diesel-engined track-layer that runs on caterpillar tracks can haul a train of sleds that together weigh 100 tons or more. But drivers may have to keep their engines running all the time to keep the fuel from freezing.

Engineers have laid railways, roads, and oil pipelines through Arctic lands. They need special skills to build on permafrost, for the topsoil is liable to heave or slide downhill.

Now, too, special ships called icebreakers can smash their way through sea ice several yards thick. Icebreakers have a strong, heavy bow, and powerful engines. The bow rears up then crushes the ice by weight. These icebreakers can keep Arctic seaways open that were once always closed in winter.

Planes and helicopters can fly to areas that are impossible to reach by land or sea. Air travel speeds miners and supplies to even the most remote oil rigs, and airliners on some long-distance flights take short cuts over Arctic lands.

Huskies pull a loaded sledge in Alaska. Dog teams have been used by the *Inuit* for many hundreds of years.

Right The British Antarctic Survey ship
RRS *Bransfield*.

Below At an Arctic village in
northern Greenland, a helicopter
prepares to lift out empty fuel drums.

Poles at risk

The *Inuit* and other Arctic peoples took only what they needed to stay alive from the land and sea. Then, greedy and thoughtless people from outside began plundering the wealth of polar regions.

Damage began more than a hundred years ago. First, European and American whalers and sealers began killing thousands of whales and fur seals to sell their oil or skins to the people back home. By the middle of this century, fast ships, spotter planes, explosive harpoons, and other equipment made mass killing easier than ever.

At times, fur seals, blue whales, and polar bears were dying faster than their young were being born. These polar mammals faced extinction.

Now, polar fish are coming under threat. Teams of small trawlers scoop up huge quantities of polar and sub-polar fish. Each team supplies a big factory ship. This stays at sea for months until its holds are full of frozen fish. Then it sails back home, perhaps to the Soviet Union-or Japan. By the mid-1980s, Soviet vacuum trawlers had sucked up 90 percent of the Antarctic cod around the sub-Antarctic island of South Georgia. Krill is also being fished, but the more krill caught for human food, the fewer there remain for fish, whales, and penguins.

Disturbance is another problem. The many tourists now visiting polar lands have damaged colonies of breeding birds. Snow machines have scarred wild stretches of Alaskan tundra. Half jokingly, someone has even said that parts of the ocean of Antarctica are paved with cans thrown overboard from ships.

One of the worst risks could come from Arctic oil wells and oil pipelines. A big oil spill might poison rivers, lakes, or the sea. Huge tracts of fragile tundra vegetation might die, along with thousands of the reindeer that cross it on migration. Arctic regions already suffer from pollution. In 1986, an explosion at the Soviet nuclear power station at Chernobyl resulted in radioactive contamination of the Arctic regions of Scandinavia and the Soviet Union. Thousands of reindeer have had to be slaughtered, which has drastically affected the lives of the nomadic reindeer-herding peoples in these areas.

Left Thousands of reindeer live in Arctic regions. Many have already died because of pollution.

Top right A major oil spill could destroy this beautiful Canadian tundra landscape.

Bottom right Polar regions are now beginning to attract tourists.

Saving the Poles

People have seen the dangers facing the world's frozen wildernesses. Now, caring groups are saving threatened polar creatures and are working hard to stop new damage from being done.

Oil companies set their own safeguards to prevent oil spills from damaging the Arctic sea or land. But some fishermen and hunters have had to be persuaded to reduce their catch of threatened fish and mammals.

Daring members of the Greenpeace conservation group have sailed small boats between the whalers and their prey. Greenpeace people have also landed on sea ice to spray seal pups with dye. This made their skins unusable for coats, so hunters spared the seal pups' lives.

But individual campaigners can do little — only nations can make laws preventing polar animals from being hunted to extinction. By 1974 Arctic nations agreed to stop killing polar bears. That year the world's whaling nations banned the killing of endangered blue, right, and humpback whales. Later, Japan agreed to stop whaling altogether. In 1983 most Western European countries stopped buying harp and hooded seal pup skins. The following year, Canadian seal hunters clubbed to death only one-tenth as many pups as usual.

As long ago as 1959, twelve nations signed an Antarctic Treaty. This set aside their claims to Antarctic lands for thirty years, and preserved Antarctica for scientific research. More nations have signed since. In 1972, sealing nations stopped killing two kinds of Antarctic seal and set hunting limits for the rest. By the mid-1980s scientists were learning how much Antarctic fish and krill could be fished without robbing penguins, seals, and whales of food.

But as the time span of the Antarctic Treaty runs out, conservationists have demanded new, strong laws to save Antarctica from damage done by mining and overfishing. Back in 1960 the United States formed the Arctic National Wildlife Range to protect much of northern Alaska. Now conservationists want the nations of the world to make Antarctica the first world wildlife park.

Left Members of the Greenpeace conservation group confront Soviet whaling ships.

Right An ornithologist weighs young shag chicks on one of the islands off Antarctica.

Below These polar bears have been temporarily anaesthetized so that scientists can carry out tests. They want to find out more about the way the bears have adapted to their harsh environment.

A glacier meets the icy waters of the Magdalena Fjord in Spitzbergen.

Glossary

Antarctic The cold lands and seas of the world's far south.

Antarctica The huge frozen island continent in the Antarctic.

Antarctic Circle An imaginary circle around the world, 66° 32' south of the equator.

Antarctic Convergence The northern edge of the Antarctic, where cold Antarctic ocean water meets warmer water from the tropics.

Antarctic Treaty An agreement made by twelve nations in 1959 to set aside their claims to Antarctica for thirty years.

Arctic The cold lands and seas of the world's far north.

Arctic Circle An imaginary circle around the world, 66° 32' north of the equator.

Arête A sharp, knife-edged mountain ridge caused by the effects of frost and glaciation.

Aurora A curtain of light produced by electricity high in the atmosphere and seen in polar regions. In the Arctic it is called the aurora borealis or northern lights. In the Antarctic it is called the aurora australis.

Blizzard A storm of powdery snow, whipped up by the wind.

Cirque A steep-sided hollow in mountainous areas originally formed by the head of a glacier; also called a corrie.

Crevasse A deep crack across or along a glacier.

Drumlin A long hill shaped like half an egg. Drumlins were shaped by ancient sheets of moving ice.

Esker A long ridge of sand and gravel: the old bed of a stream that flowed beneath a glacier or ice sheet.

Fjord A long narrow coastal inlet with steep sides. Fjords were carved by valley glaciers that later melted.

Glacier A river of ice.

Hanging valley A valley high up the side of a large glaciated valley. It marks the point where a small glacier joined a much larger glacier.

Ice Age A time when ice covers a large part of the Earth's surface.

Iceberg A large chunk of land ice floating in the sea. Icebergs are broken bits of glaciers and ice shelves.

Icebreaker A strongly-built ship designed to smash a path through thick sea ice.

Ice cap A mass of ice and snow covering an island or mountain area.

Ice sheet A huge mass of ice and snow. Ice sheets cover most of Antarctica and Greenland.

Ice shelf A huge sheet of floating ice attached to land. Antarctica's Ross Ice Shelf is bigger than Japan.

Inuit The proper name for Eskimos.

Mirage An effect of light that makes objects seem to be in places where they are not. Mirages occur where light is bent by passing through layers of air at different temperatures.

Moraine A mass of broken rock moved by a glacier or ice sheet.

Northeast Passage The Arctic sea route around northern Europe and north Asia.

Northwest Passage The Arctic sea route around northern North America.

Nunatak A sharp mountain peak projecting through an ice cap or ice sheet.

Ornithologist Someone who studies birds.

Pack ice Large blocks of sea ice wedged together in a huge mass.

Pancake ice Thin, flat, rounded cakes of ice that form as the sea freezes.

Permafrost Ground that is always frozen.

Pingo A hillock pushed up by a plug of ice that forms below an empty lake.

Poles Imaginary points at the world's farthest north and south. They mark the ends of the earth's axis, a straight line around which the earth revolves.

Polynya A strip of open water in sea ice.

Scree A sloping heap of weathered rock fragments.

Snout The end of a glacier.

Snowmobile A small, powered machine with runners, for speeding over snow.

Tree line The farthest north, or the highest point on a mountain where full-sized trees will grow.

Tundra Treeless plains of Arctic Europe, Asia, and North America.

Further reading

Asimov, Isaac, *How Did We Find Out About Antarctica?* (Walker & Co., 1979).

Barrett, Ian, *Tundra and People* (Silver Burdett Press, 1982).

Bromwell, Martin, *Glaciers and Icecaps* (Franklin Watts, 1986).

Culsin, Michel, *The Frozen North* (Silver Burdett Press, 1985).

Finney, Susan and Kindle, Patricia, *Antarctic Explorations* (Good Apple 1985).

Fordham, Derek, *Eskimos* (Silver Burdett Press, 1979).

Green, Christopher, *Polar Lands* (Merrimack, 1984).

Hargreaves, Pat, *The Antarctic* (Silver Burdett Press, 1980)

Hargreaves, Pat, *The Arctic* (Silver Burdett Press, 1981).

Johnson, Sylvia A., *Animals of the Polar Regions* (Lerner Publications, 1976).

Sandak, Cass,R.,*The Arctic and Antarctic* (Franklin Watts,1985).

Sovle, Gardner, *Antarctica* (Franklin Watts, 1985).

Picture acknowledgments

The publishers would like to thank the following for allowing their photographs to be reproduced in this book: Bryan and Cherry Alexander 5, 9, 21 (bottom), 29, 30, 31, 39 (top), 41 (bottom), back cover; British Antarctic Survey 34 (D.D. Wynn Williams); Bruce Coleman Limited 11 (Francisco Erize), 12 (top/Steven Kaufman), 13 (Robert Burton), 19 (Robert Burton), 21 (top), 25 (Bruce Lankinen), 40 (Bryan and Cherry Alexander), 41 (top/Bob and Clara Calhoun), front cover main picture (WWF/Y.J. Rey-Millet); GeoScience Features Picture Library 12 (bottom), 14, 39 (bottom); Greenpeace 42; Oxford Scientific Films 4 (Andrew Lister), 15 (David C. Fritts), 17 (both/Doug Allan), 20 (Andrew Lister), 23 (top/Christian B. Hvidt), 23 (bottom/Doug Allan), 26 (Doug Leszczynski), 27 (Brian Milne), 28 (Doug Allan), 43 (top/Doug Allan), front cover inset (E. Degginger); Royal Geographical Society 33 (bottom left and right), 35; Wayland Picture Library 33 (top), 36; ZEFA 7, 37 (top/Ricatto), 37 (bottom/McCutcheon), 38 (Steenmans), 43 (bottom/ P.W. Bading), 44 (R. Everts). All illustrations are by Stefan Chabluk with the exception of the following: 22 (Cliff Meadway); 9, 24–25 (Wendy Meadway).

Index

Alaska 6, 12, 15, 20, 36–7, 38, 42
Amundsen, Roald 32, 34–5
Animals 5, 24–5, 26, 28, 32, 40, 42–3
Antarctica 4–10, 16–18, 20, 22–3,
   28, 31, 34–6, 38, 40, 42–3
Antarctic Circle 4, 7, 8
Antarctic Convergence 7
Antarctic ice sheet 10, 16, 20, 34
Antarctic Treaty 42
Arctic Circle 4, 6, 8
Arctic fox 24–5
Arctic ground squirrel 24
Arctic hare 24–5
Arctic National Wildlife Range 42
Arctic Ocean 6, 16–17, 20, 26, 32
Arctic peoples 30–31, 40
Arctic regions 4–6, 8, 10, 12–14,
   16–18, 20–26, 32, 36, 37, 40, 42
Arêtes 12
Asia 6, 8, 32, 36
Atlantic Ocean 6–7, 20, 36
Aurora australis 21
Aurora borealis 21
Australia 34
Autumn 18

Beluga 26
Birds 24–5, 28, 40, 42–3
British Commonwealth Expedition 34
British Isles 8, 34
Byrd, Richard 32, 34

Canada 6, 8, 14, 18, 20, 23, 31, 32,
   36, 41, 42
Caribou 24–5, 31 (*also see* Reindeer)
Chernobyl 40
Chile 34
Cirques 13
Climate 4–5, 7, 8, 16, 18–21, 24, 32,
   34
Conservation 42

Cook, James 34–5
Crevasses 10

Davis, John 34
Dogs 31, 32, 34, 38
Drumlins 13

Erratics 13
Eskers 13
Eskimos, *see Inuit*
Europe 6, 8, 30, 32–3, 36, 40, 42
Explorers, Antarctic 34–5
   Arctic 32–3

Factory ships 40
Fast ice 16
Finland 6
Fish 25, 26, 28, 36, 38, 40, 42
Fjords 13, 44
Forests 14, 24–5
Frobisher, Martin 33
Frost 5, 12–13, 14, 22
Fuchs, Vivien 34–5

Gas 36
Glaciation 12–13
Glaciers 10–13, 17, 44
Greenland 6–7, 8, 10, 12, 14, 17,
   18–19, 23, 31, 32–3, 36, 39
Greenland ice sheet 10, 18
Greenpeace 42

Hanging valleys 13
Hudson Bay 6
Hunting 34–5, 36, 38, 42
Huskies 38

Ice 5, 6–7, 8, 10, 12, 14, 16–18, 21,
   28, 30, 32, 34, 36, 38
Ice age 8
Icebergs 17, 21

Icebreakers 32, 28
Ice caps 8, 10
Iceland 36
Ice sheets 8, 10, 12–13, 14, 16, 18,
   20–21, 34
Ice shelves 10, 17, 28
Ichthyostega 8
Igloos 30–31
Indian Ocean 7
Insects 25, 28
Inuit 7, 30–31, 32, 38, 40

Japan 36, 40, 42

Kayaks 7, 31
Krill 26, 28, 36, 40, 42

Lapps 28–9, 37, 40
Lemmings 24–5
Lystrosaurus 8–9

Magnetic poles 4
Midnight sun 19
Migration 25, 40
Minerals 32, 36
Mining 36, 38, 42
Moraine 12–13
Mountains 12–13, 15
Mount McKinley 15
Musk oxen 24

Nansen, Fridtjof 32
New Zealand 34
Nordenskjold, Nils 32
North America 6, 8, 14–15, 18, 20,
   23, 24, 31, 32, 36, 42
Northeast Passage 32
Northern lights 21
North Pole 4–5, 8, 16, 18, 32
Northwest Passage 32–3
Norway 6, 32, 34

Novaya Zemlya 10
Nunataks 10, 12

Ocean currents 6, 8, 16–17, 32
Oil 36–7, 38, 40, 42

Pacific Ocean 6–7, 20
Pack ice 6, 7, 16, 18, 26
Pancake ice 16–17
Peary, Robert 32–3
Penguins 28–9, 40, 42
    Adélie 28
    emperor 28
    gentoo 28–9
Permafrost 14, 22
Petroleum 36
Pingos 14
Pipelines 37, 38, 40
Plankton 26
Plants 5, 14–15, 22–6, 40–41
Polar bears 26, 31, 41, 42–3
Polar regions, formation of 8
    limits of 4, 6–7
Pollution 40
Polynyas 16
Prehistoric life 8–9
Ptarmigan 24
Pyramidal peaks 12–13

Reindeer 24, 30, 36, 40 (also see
    Caribou)
Research bases 20, 34

Samoyeds 30–31
Sandhill cranes 24
Sastrugi 10
Satellites 32
Scandinavia 6, 8, 30, 32, 34, 36, 40
Scientists 6, 8, 14, 31, 32, 34,

Scott, Robert Falcon 34–5
Scree 12
Sea ice 9, 16, 18, 32, 38
Sealers 36, 40
Seals 17, 26, 28, 31, 34, 36, 40, 42
    crabeater 17, 28
    elephant 28
    fur 40
    harp 42
    hooded 42
    leopard 28
    Ross 28
    Weddell 28
Seasons 18–21
Ships 32–3, 36, 38–9
Shore leads 16
Siberia 18, 20
Sledges 31, 32, 34, 38
Snow 5, 8, 10, 14, 18, 20–21, 22,
    24–5, 30, 38
Snowy owls 24
Soils 14, 22
Southern Ocean 7
South Georgia 40
South Pole 4–5, 8, 18, 34–5
Soviet Union 6, 8, 10, 14, 30, 32, 34,
    36, 40
Spitzbergen 10, 44
Spring 18, 25
Stoats 24–5
Submarines 32
Summer 5, 8, 14, 18–19, 20, 22–3
Sun 4–5, 18–19, 20, 22
Sweden 6, 30, 32

Till 13
Tourists 40–41
Trans-Antarctic Expedition 34–5
Transportation 32, 34, 38–9
Tree line 6
Trees 6, 22

Tundra 14–15, 16, 18, 22, 25, 28, 36
    40–41
Tundra voles 25

United States 6, 8, 12, 15, 20, 34,
    36–7, 38, 42
U.S.S.R. see Soviet Union

Valleys 12–13

Walrus 26–7
Weasels 24–5
Weather see Climate
Whalers 36, 40, 42
Whales 26, 31, 36, 40, 42
    blue 26, 40, 42
    humpback 42
    killer 26
    right 42
    white 26
Whistling swans 24
Wilkes, Charles 34–5
Winter 4–5, 6, 8, 18–21, 22, 24–5,
    28, 31, 38
Wolverines 24
Wolves 24

Yakuts 30–31